Embracing
the Wild Magick
OF BEing

By
Leigh Heasley

Published by True Beginnings Publishing.
Copyright 2021 by Leigh Heasley.

Empower
The Wild Magick Of BEing

$\mathcal{E}$ach of us are on incomparable journeys of SELF-realization. Truths are universal but must be discovered and rediscovered in our own way. The culmination of these experiences sparks a remembering of the Masters we inherently are, which I deem BEing Wild Magick.

Connecting with and living my truth became imperative after I had our daughter in 2004. My world was turned upside down. Not only was I a new mother, but my body began failing me in ways the doctors could not explain. I had to let go of my own expectations and those others may have had of me. Asking for and receiving help was the first important step. Then I had to learn to trust my instincts of what felt right and what didn't. Next was learning to say *no* because of a tendency to undervalue my time.

With my needs met, healthy boundaries with relationships and circumstances became easier to define. This allowed me the opportunity to focus on my wellness. I delved into energy work, crystals, herbs, oils, and yoga. I had immediate positive results. While metaphysics, esoteric practices, shamanism, druidism and mysticism helped me form a deeper relationship with myself and something greater, journaling and free writing allowed me to consciously actualize what I was learning. Age old wisdom became a tangible presence giving me daily clarity, purpose, and direction.

I began to understand that nothing was absolute, everything was relative, and there was a reason for it all, even if I couldn't understand it at that moment. If I worked on myself and focused on what was in my power to change, nurture, and grow, then I would thrive. In turn, I could be fully present for my family, friends, and community to support the kind of world I dreamt of.

It has taken years to cultivate a healthy and content life, yet the benefits of my original shift in thinking back in 2004 were felt within that first year. There have been plenty of challenges along the way. Some were brought on by choice and others because of outside influences. All of which have aided my growth and added a fullness I never knew I was missing. With practice, the power to influence the direction of my life grows. I hope you have felt this to be true for yourself, and if not, may you begin to feel so in days to come.

In this book are curated materials taken from my own journey that helped promote self-sovereignty. In addition, you will find a selection of ideas from previously published books that have been reworked to reflect how I understand them now. The original books can be purchased on Amazon. More spiritual tools and materials can be found on my website (http://lei629.wix.com/empower). No matter the path you take, I hope what I share is beneficial. Remember, what resonates, keep. Let the rest fall away.

What
It Means To Be HUman?

1) You are a bridge between the expansion and contraction of energy.

2) You are a vessel of constant alchemical transmutations, within and without.

3) You are a weaver from BEyond, living in material form.

You have the ability to develop your senses and transform your experiences indefinitely; co-creating endings, beginnings, and all things in between until you get your fill.

You are in a space of possibility, potential, and plausibility that allows you all the benefits of this physical form, plus access to other realms of spirit to manifest your soul's desire.

Large collective shifts begin first with the individual. Each of us has something special to offer. Together we usher in a new reality of co-creative bliss and consciously shared responsibility.

The
Inner Wayshower

*K*nowing yourself doesn't mean uncovering a final answer but instead cultivating a relationship with the undercurrent of your subconscious. You are invited to wade in these unknown waters during spiritual practice, meditation, or just listening to your intuition closely as you mindfully go about your day.

As long as you surrender, The Inner Wayshower will take you down the spiral and back out. Traversing unexplored territory of your psyche, there are clues to be found that affirm your deepest yearnings. Pay attention to signs, synchronicities, and your senses.

Being honest about what you find takes courage. You may not be able to cross the threshold of full awareness until you have made holistic life preparations to accommodate a shift in your perceptions. The everyday life implications can be jarring at first. It may take several attempts to fully understand the scope and breadth of what is brought to light. Reflection and contemplation are necessary to bring awareness to your progress. Get comfortable with testing your limits.

Labels
As Accessories

*P*lease consider...

What if you used labels as accessories, nothing more or less?...

What if you could slip from one to the next without being confined by them, instead reinventing each one adding your own flare, definitions, and parameters to enhance our BEing...

What if you saw naming as a form of play, a jumping off point for our creativity instead of a way to cause separation?...

What if you used identification only for the sake of poetic verse to inspire meaning instead of a way to categorize?...

What if you used denotation as a challenge, a test of your mind's flexibility and heart's openness to see how far you can bend your version of reality, instead of submitting to the generally agreed upon one?

Treat
Yourself With Kindness

*Y*ou deserve beauty, special care, and immersion in life's bounty. The degree of your wholeness is reflected in our experiences, inward and outward.

When you neglect your wellness, it manifests as sickness, stress, and suffering. Remove what does not offer balance. Focus on the things that embolden your spirit.

Keep it simple. Be real with yourself. You are what this world needs, just as you are.

Your Life
In Review

*H*ere is a checklist to build awareness in your life. Keeping track of your physical, emotional, mental, and spiritual health are the keys to unfolding your potential.

1.) Do you live in a stable environment?

    a. being financially secure

    b. nurturing solid relationships

    c. feeling worthy and important

2.) Do you participate in the joy of living?

    a. having healthy sexual and sensual experiences

    b. taking part in activities that make you happy

    c. flowing with and not controlling life

3.) Do you know your purpose, and are you acting upon
   it?
   a. letting yourself dream and aspire
   b. being focused and dedicated
   c. leading with your experience and talents

4.) Do you know how to unconditionally love yourself and
   others?
   a. acknowledging imbalances mentally, emotionally, or
      physically
   b. enacting discernment for proper boundaries
   c. keeping your center amongst change

5.) Do you speak your truth and allow others to speak
   theirs?
   a. knowing when to speak up, when to listen, and when
      to keep silent
   b. understanding how you present yourself
   c. navigating your life with grace

6.) Do you trust your ability to discern?

    a. connecting with your archetypes (the roles you play in life)

    b. implementing knowledge to see life with clarity

    c. trusting intuition & inner guidance

7.) Do you feel connected to something bigger than yourself?

    a. cultivating wisdom (knowledge in practice)

    b. exploring a personal spiritual path and/or self-actualization

    c. making choices based on the understanding of interconnectedness

Rewrite
Your Destiny

*F*rom the start, you are conditioned and defined by relationships with the external world; family, friends, community. You filtered that through whatever awareness you brought with you into this life from birth and beyond. At some point during your evolution of SELF, you will feel a need to transcend who you thought you were to become more of who you might yet become. The following writing exercises are meant to kindle your abilities to conceptualize and actualize.

This first part will require vibrant unadulterated imagination. As you write, let it flow. Literally, don't interrupt with thoughts of doubt, judgment, or disbelief. Be as whimsical as your heart desires. You might find yourself writing about past lives or distant futures on other planets. Maybe you will expand upon a childhood dream to explore what happened if you would have followed through. This may also be a way to give yourself permission to be someone completely new. If you could start fresh with no restrictions and unlimited resources, what would your life look like? This should be fun and freeing; a way to get you in touch with your creativity.

The next part may be a little more challenging, but necessary. Begin at the beginning, from childhood to present day. This is a way to acknowledge your past to heal, honor how far you have come, and hopefully give you excitement for what is to come. It is important to be transparent. The more detail you recall, the better equipped you will be to move forward. Note the good, bad, and everything in-between that reveals strengths, weaknesses, and potential. You need to know the specifics so you can gain wisdom about where you came from, where you are now, and how you will be able to go in a different direction from here.

The final part is to make a list of future wants and current needs. Prioritize. Begin mapping out long term, medium, and short-term goals. Stay practical yet flexible. Nurture fresh ideas. Allow others to support you. Keep your distance from anyone or anything that might lead you astray.

Clearing The Old
To Make Room For The New

A practice of gratitude lets the universe know you are ready for more beauty, abundance, and joy. What are you grateful for? What do you love and appreciate about your life? Who lifts you up and helps you remember who you are? These are just a few. You deserve a life overflowing with blessings. Your power of co-creation depends on right focus, right intention, and right desire.

You are what you expose yourself to. You are your choices; people, places, situations, entertainment, education, jobs, and so on. Every detail of your life matters. You have a set amount of energy. It is precious. How do you intend to spend it? Don't let conditioning, obligations, or distractions keep you from living your truth.

You have a world of possibilities available to you, but it requires courage, flexibility, determination, and creativity. The new can only present itself when the old has been acknowledged, healed, and released. Allow yourself to dream. Be eager and willing to continually reinvent.

Love your body. Stay connected to nature. Meditate and reflect. Tread lightly on the earth for future generations. Appreciate that less is more. Keep your life uncluttered physically, mentally, and emotionally. Surround yourself with beauty. Never stop learning. Remember to breathe.

Building Confident
Communication Skills

$\mathcal{F}$eeling heard or properly hearing someone else is a simple matter if you can remove emotions and perceptions. Emotions are those subjective feelings you get when something doesn't resonate with you. They override the rational mind. Perceptions are built upon past experiences. They both skew how you understand the situation.

How to move beyond emotions and perceptions takes some practice. You need tools so that you may express yourself in a calm, detached, and straight-forward manner. First is to mutually decide on a time and place to have a private exchange. The basic rules of engagement should include refraining from speaking in circles, raising voice levels, interrupting, bringing up the past, name calling, and aggressive statements.

Do not be afraid to walk away to calm down before revisiting the subject. Also, keep to sentences starting with *I feel* and *I need*. Focus on your side of the story. Don't make assumptions about the other person. Let them speak for themselves. Take turns. Repeat what you heard back to the person to make sure you are hearing them correctly, and then respond.

Sometimes it is better not to speak. Write it out instead; again, still using the rules of engagement. Writing gives you the opportunity to connect with what you are processing and what you need to say, removing yourself from impulsive reactions to the situation.

Please always confront your feelings and speak up when you are inspired to do so. Bottling these up will bring unnecessary stress and create an environment of disharmony. This is reflected in your physical body and environment. What you have to say is important, always. Being afraid of conflict prolongs the inevitable confrontation. Much relief is to be had once it is out in the open for both parties.

Remember that it is okay to disagree. There is no winner or loser, just two people wanting to be heard and understood.

If it is a major issue that can't be worked through in this way, please get a nonpartisan mediator. In the workplace, it could be a trusted co-worker, manager, or someone from human resources. At home, ask for help from a relative, friend, or therapist.

There are three sides to every story; one person, the second person, and the truth. Hold compassion in your heart, trust your judgment, and stand strong in your truths. We have nothing to prove but much to understand.

Finding Peace
Where You Are

There is no need to take your life's challenges head on. It is probably better not to. The best time to make lasting change is when you are able to see clearly. How can you reflect if your mind is not quiet? We can't begin to analyze our lives until we first make peace within it. Here is a non-invasive, loving approach to healing right where you are.

When you rise before you get out of bed recite the Serenity Prayer:

"Grant me the serenity to accept the things I cannot change; courage to change the things I can; and wisdom to know the difference."

-Drink an 8oz glass of filtered water that is room temperature or warmed on the stove, with lemon or lime.

(plain water is okay too) This flushes the toxins from the body and prepares it for digestion.

-Then take a 15-minute walk in nature. After your walk, write in a journal. Document, thoughts, feelings, insight, or just a word that represents you in the moment.

-Mindfully prepare for the day ahead as you take some deep breaths.

-Be patient, tolerant, and compassionate with yourself and others.

-It's OK to say NO. You are most useful when your needs are met first. When depleted, you are not able to give 100%.

-Remind yourself that eating and drinking are not secondary needs. They are primary. Give them the attention they deserve. Offer thanks and reverence. While consuming, give your undivided attention to the process. Connect with all your senses as you enjoy this time of nurturing.

-At least once a day, do something that makes you happy like taking a hot shower or bath with your favorite scented products, lighting candles and playing pretty music, dance or sing along with music that makes you feel alive, watch your favorite movie or tv show, or read a book.

-When the day is done and bedtime is eminent, begin light stretching to release accumulated tension from your body.

When you are ready to lie down, find a position that feels supportive. Close your eyes. Let your body feel heavy. Take a few deep breaths. Offer up your worries, troubles, or doubts to a higher power, angels, ancestors, guides, or nature spirits. They will gladly bear your burdens so you can sleep deeply.

As you begin this journey of self-sovereignty, please ask a friend to join you. It is always best to have support so you can practice accountability and maintain momentum. Require the highest good for each other, focusing on the positive and offering objective insight. You deserve a soulful life.

Daily
Centering

$\mathcal{F}$ind a quiet place free from distractions. Sit or lie down comfortably. Clear your mind. Breathe deeply. Imagine yourself as a great tree that grows roots into the Earth and branches that reach into the Heavens. Envision a golden white light traveling from the tips of your branches, moving through your trunk, then anchoring within the heart of the Earth. Ask that this column of light be with you day and night and in all the space in-between, bringing deep peace to all facets of your life. When you have finished, take a few moments to slowly bring awareness back to your physical body. Know that your spirit is constant and shining brightly, always.

Affirmations

I am a being of nature.

I am provided for.

I am important.

I am filled with wonder.

I trust my feelings.

I am beautiful.

I am responsible for my life.

I am determined.

I am powerful.

I am at peace with my life.

I accept myself as I am.

I am loved.

I connect with the deeper meaning of my experiences.

I express my truth.

I am creative.

I am a seeker of wisdom.

I trust my intuition.

I am intelligent.

I see the Divine in everything.

I live a life of purpose.

I am Divine.

Isms

*Time + Attention + Money = Reality

*Be humble but never forget your power.

*Live as though the world is exactly the way you wish.

*There are no offenses, only experiences.

*Peace is non-negotiable. Be present. Heed inner
   knowing.

*Follow your own rhythms, your own flow, regardless of
   what the rest of the world is doing.

*We do not need to eradicate the ego, only to embrace it.
   (self + SELF = WHOLENESS)

*Always there is coming and going; The eternal movement of life.

*Collective reality shifts when enough people believe in the same dream.

*Imagination, intuition, instincts, innocence, and insight are necessary for sustainable change.

*Put theory into practice, keep/reject hypotheses, repeat. Order directs Chaos.

*EveryTHING is a code to be translated and understood relative to our own experience.

Distillations
From Awaking Beings Of Light, The Living Web, & I AM

-Trust that you are adaptable and capable of walking through the ever-revolving doors of perception. Nothing is secret. All is hidden in plain sight.

-Everything continually needs to be rediscovered, reevaluated, and redefined. It is the process of creation and destruction that brings understanding, healing, integration, and expansion.

-A quiet mind does not mean an empty mind. Instead, it is a state of receptivity.

-Chaos is an indicator of higher laws at work.

-Illumination may be interpreted in many ways depending on our ability to handle the truth. What you seek may not be what you were expecting. You must be willing to drop everything you know to understand it.

-Do not be consumed by the idea of Oneness. Otherwise, you may pass up opportunities to explore all facets of life.

-Bliss is a way of experiencing the world. Each day, each moment, each sensation, and each breath is a spiritual phenomenon. No clinging. No offenses. No errors. Witness and engage as you choose with nothing to lose and everything to gain. Celebrate the spectrum of your BEingness.

-Remember, unconditional love does not guarantee unconditional like. Uphold healthy boundaries. Drop expectations. Love in a way that honors mutual respect and growth.

-The more aware you become the less likely you are to accept the current reality. What kind of web are you weaving? Does it support harmony? Does it reflect the world you desire to experience? Educate. Meditate. Act.

-Raw energy is undefinable, abundant, and pervasive. Once coalesced around a thought, it becomes denser. A form will emerge after prolonged attention and heightened emotion. There is power in choice.

-Imagination is a catalyst for change. Nonattachment is creative freedom. Commitment to your vision will manifest it.

-Hold the feeling of your dream being realized. Don't let your mind get stuck in the *how*. Believe that everything will fall into place as it needs to. Let the universe guide you in the form of synchronicities and signs.

-Trust your heart. Condition your mind. Keep your focus. Mindfully choose. These are building blocks for soulful living.

-The outer world is a reflection of the inner world. Compassion for all of life charges us with the responsibility for Self-Mastery.

-Pain is a reminder that you are misaligned and out of touch with some part of yourself. Remember, there are no offenses, only projections of the mind. Offer prayers of gratitude for all that is perfect right this moment, to begin the process of re-attunement. Happiness, contentment, and peace must be nurtured.

-Be careful not to compare or judge using preconditioning. Instead, observe and contemplate in accordance with your own desired world view. How do your findings relate to the present standards? Does it reinforce or invalidate? Use beliefs, ideas, and concepts for their usefulness. Let them fall away once their purpose has been fulfilled.

-Duality is relative, a tool for us to measure experience. Be open to the beauty of life. Embrace the light and shadow, for this is the dance of Spirit in form.

-Innocence brings you back to your intended state of BEing. Continue finding new ways to be inspired. See the common, usual, and mundane with eyes of wonder. Be curious. Be amazed.

-You are weaving and unweaving your portion of the collective web with each decision you make. Are you creating new patterns or strengthening the old? Have the courage to be unique and step outside your comfort zone. If enough people do the same, we can redesign the tapestry of our shared experience.

Dream the unimaginable.
Believe in the impossible.
What moves you deeply
has the power to transform.

About the Author

Leigh Heasley is a soulful living advocate. She spends her days enjoying time with her family, nature, and all forms of art. Leigh uses online platforms to share many facets of her life to build a community of authenticity, creativity, and mindfulness. She believes that together we can courageously explore who we are and who we might yet become.

Find out more about Leigh on her website!
http://lei629.wix.com/empower

Made in the USA
Middletown, DE
24 August 2024

59666046R10026